29.90
RF

Heinemann
First
Encyclopedia

Volume 8
Pte-Slo

Heinemann Library
Chicago, Illinois

© 1999 Reed Educational & Professional Publishing
Published by Heinemann Library,
an imprint of Reed Educational & Professional Publishing,
Chicago, IL 60602
Customer Service 888-454-2279
Visit our website at www.heiniemannlibrary.com

Series Editors: Rebecca and Stephen Vickers
Author Team: Rob Alcraft, Catherine Chambers, Jim Drake,
Fred Martin, Angela Royston, Jane Shuter, Roger Thomas,
Rebecca Vickers, Stephen Vickers

Photo research by Katharine Smith
Designed and Typeset by Gecko Ltd
Printed in Hong Kong, China

03 02 01 00
10 9 8 7 6 5 4 3 2

Library of Congress Cataloging-in-Publication Data

Heinemann first encyclopedia.
     p.   cm.
     Summary: A ten-volume encyclopedia covering animals, plants,
countries, transportation, science, ancient civilizations, and world
history.
     ISBN 1-57572-741-2 (lib. bdg.)
     1. Children's encyclopedias and dictionaries. [1. Encyclopedias
and dictionaries.] I. Heinemann Library (Firm)
AG5.H45   1998
031—dc21
                                      98-20016
                                         CIP
                                         AC

Acknowledgments

Cover: The cover illustration is of a male specimen of Ornithoptera goliath, commonly called the Goliath Birdwing. Special thanks
to Dr. George C. McGavin and the Hope Entomological Collections, Oxford University Museum of Natural History; J. Allan
Cash Ltd., pp. 13 left; 21 bottom, 25, 27, 29, 41 bottom, 42, 44, 47, 48; British Museum, p. 30 right; Bruce Coleman Ltd./Dr
Eckart Pott, p. 8 top; EPS Press, p. 11 bottom; Forest Life Picture Library, p. 30 left; The Hutchison Library, pp.18 top, 26, 43
bottom; L. Taylor, p 43 top; Kobal Collection, p. 20 top; Mansell Collection, p. 11 top; Natural History Museum/Mary Anning, p.
4; Oxford Scientific Film/Harold Taylor Abipp, p. 8 bottom; Doug Allan, p. 37 top; G.I. Bernard, p. 8 bottom; Martyn Colbeck,
p. 34 top; J.A.L. Cook, p. 28 bottom; Mary Deebie and Victoria Stone, p. 34 bottom; Warren Faidley, p. 12 bottom; Carol
Farnetti, p. 14 bottom; David Fritts, p. 17 bottom; Peter Gathercole, p. 18 bottom; Howard Hall, p. 15 bottom; Richard Hermann,
p. 35 bottom; Rudie Kuiter, p. 32; Zig Leszczynski, p. 9 bottom; C.K. Lorenz, p. 9 top; T.C. Middleston, p. 21 top; Sean Morris, p.
13 right; William Paton, p. 8 top; Press-Tige Pictures, p. 14 bottom; Richard Ray, p. 46 top; L.L.T. Rhodes, p. 40 bottom; James
Robinson, p. 36 right; Norbert Rosing, p. 37 bottom; Kjell Sandved, p. 35 top; Wendy Shattil and Bob Rozinski, p. 46 bottom;
David Tipling, p. 36 left; Steve Turner, p. 17 top; Tom Ulrich, p. 41 top; P. and W. Ward, p. 28 top; Barrie Watts, p. 31 top;
Doug Wechsler, p. 31 bottom; Babs and Bert Wells, p. 16 bottom; Robert Wu, p. 33 top; Picturepoint, p. 6 bottom; Science Photo
Library, p. 45 bottom; John Mead, p. 10 top; Still Pictures/John Concalori, p.16 top; Tony Stone Worldwide/Simeone Huber, p.
7; Gavriel Jecan, p. 22; Werner Forman Archive. p. 6 top; Zefa, p. 19 bottom.

Welcome to
Heinemann First Encyclopedia

What is an encyclopedia?

An encyclopedia is an information book. It gives the most important facts about many different subjects. This encyclopedia has been written for children who are using an encyclopedia for the first time. It covers many of the subjects from school and others you may find interesting.

What is in this encyclopedia?

In this encyclopedia, each topic is called an *entry*. There is one page of information for every entry. The entries in this encyclopedia explain

- animals
- plants
- dinosaurs
- countries
- geography
- history
- world religions
- music
- art
- transportation
- science
- technology

How to use this encyclopedia

This encyclopedia has eleven books called *volumes*. The first ten volumes contain entries. The entries are all in alphabetical order. This means that Volume 1 starts with entries that begin with the letter *A* and Volume 10 ends with entries that begin with the letter *Z*. Volume 11 is the index volume. It also has interesting information about American history.

Here are two entries that show you what you can find on a page:

The "see also" *line tells you where to find other related information.*

This is the letter that the entry starts with.

Fact boxes give you details about the topic.

Did You Know? *boxes have fun or interesting bits of information.*

The Fact File *tells you important facts and figures.*

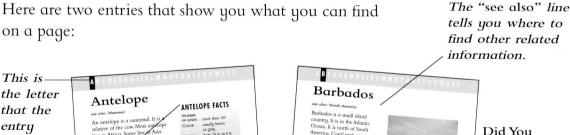

Pterosaur

see also: Dinosaur, Fossil

The pterosaurs were flying lizards.
They lived at the time of the
dinosaurs. They had leathery wings.
They did not have feathers. Their
long, bony tails helped them steer.
There were many kinds of pterosaur.

Lifestyle

Some pterosaurs were small and fast flying.
The pterodactyl was a small pterosaur. Other
pterosaurs were giants. Their wings were 23
feet across. They were as big as a small
airplane. The giant pteranodon could swoop
down. It could scoop up fish from rivers or
lakes. Pterodactyls may have also
been able to catch
flying insects.

FACTS

COLOR .... not known
SIZE .... from 8 inches to 36 feet
WEIGHT ... up to 55 lbs.
BIGGEST ... Quetzalcoatlus–36 feet
long

long fourth finger
to hold the
leathery wing

*a Rhamphorhynchus
pterosaur*

long, bony tail for
steering

fourth finger

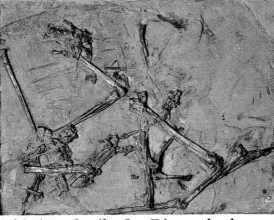

*This is a fossil of a Dimorphodon
pterosaur. It shows the long fourth
finger bone.*

INSECT AND MEAT EATER

*Pterosaurs had rows of spiky teeth. This
helped them to catch fish and insects.*

Puerto Rico

see also: North America,
United States of America

Puerto Rico is a country in the Caribbean Sea. It is a group of islands. The largest island has mountains. The north and south coasts have flat land. The climate is warm, windy, and wet.

Living in Puerto Rico

Most people in Puerto Rico live in the cities and towns. They work in factories and offices. The work of some Puerto Ricans is helping tourists. Coffee, vegetables, sugar cane, rice, and bananas are grown on farms.

Puerto Ricans are a mixture of African, Spanish, and local Native Americans. Most of the people are Roman Catholic Christians. There are many colorful religious festivals and saints' days. One of the most important festivals is "Festival of Innocents." Costumes and floats are used in the celebration.

This man is wearing a special festival costume. He has won a prize.

DID YOU KNOW?

Puerto Rico has a special relationship with the United States. Its representative in the U.S. Congress can speak, but cannot vote.

NORTH AMERICA

FACT FILE

PEOPLE	Puerto Ricans
POPULATION	about 4 million
MAIN LANGUAGES	Spanish, English
CAPITAL CITY	San Juan
MONEY	U.S. dollar
HIGHEST MOUNTAIN	Cerro de Punta–4,391 feet
LONGEST RIVER	Grand de Arecibo–40 miles

Puppetry

see also: Drama, Theater

Puppetry is a way of telling stories. It uses dolls called puppets. The person who moves them is called a puppeteer.

Types of puppets

Puppets can be moved in different ways. A puppeteer might wear a glove puppet on his or her hand. Puppets can also be moved with strings or on sticks. They can even be moved electronically. Some puppets are cut from flat shapes. A light shines from behind them. These puppets appear as shadows.

The children are watching a Punch and Judy show. It is about Punch and his wife, Judy. In these stories, Punch fights with Judy, a policeman, and a crocodile. Punch fights with everyone.

How puppets are used

Puppets are often used to tell stories to children. In some countries, such as Japan, puppet shows are also for adults.

Puppets are still a popular way of telling a story. New puppet shows are performed for live audiences and for television. One famous puppeteer is Jim Henson. He created the Muppets. Another famous puppeteer is Gerry Anderson. He invented the puppets in many space adventure stories.

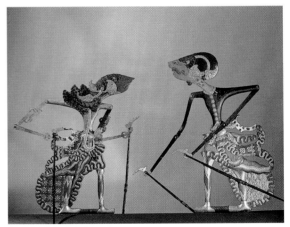

Puppets from the island of Java in Indonesia are used to tell folktales. They are moved by sticks.

DID YOU KNOW?

Puppets that hang from strings are called marionettes.

Pyramid

see also: Egypt; Egypt, Ancient; Maya

Pyramids were first made by the ancient Egyptians. They built these buildings about 4,500 years ago. The first pyramids had square bases. The sides went up to a point. They looked like steps. Later pyramids had smooth sides.

What were the pyramids?

The pyramids were huge tombs. They were built for the ancient Egyptian rulers. These rulers were called *pharaohs.* The ancient Egyptians believed people would have a life after they died. So they buried their dead with food and useful things.

The Egyptian pyramids were so well built that they are still standing.

KEY DATES

2660 B.C.	first step pyramid is built in Ancient Egypt
2600 B.C.	first smooth-sided pyramid is built in Ancient Egypt
2580 B.C.	Great Pyramid is built at Giza
1500 B.C.	ancient Egyptians begin to bury their pharaohs in tombs, not pyramids
A.D. 500	Maya build step pyramid temples

Mummies

Ancient Egyptians believed people needed their bodies after they died. So, they tried to make sure that dead bodies did not rot away. They took out the soft insides of the dead person. Next they dried out the body. Then they wrapped the body in bandages that were soaked in oil.

A body that got this special treatment was called a mummy. The dried mummy was put in a specially shaped wooden box. A face was painted on the box. The face looked like the person inside the box. This special box is called a *sarcophagus.*

DID YOU KNOW?

The Maya people of Central America built step pyramids. The pyramids were temples to their gods. People climbed the steps to get to the temple on the flat top.

Rabbit

see also: Mammal, Hare

A rabbit is a small, long-eared mammal. It is often kept as a pet. A rabbit can run very fast. Some kinds of rabbits can run as fast as 25 miles per hour. They can hop a long way in one leap. A rabbit usually sleeps in the day. It comes out at night. Rabbits live all around the world.

Rabbit families

Some kinds of rabbits live with many other rabbits. They live in large underground tunnels called a warren. Some kinds of rabbits live alone.

A male is called a buck. A female is called a doe. A baby is sometimes called a kitten or a bunny. Female rabbits have several litters each year. They have five to eight babies in each litter. Some rabbits have their babies underground. Other rabbits make nests in the grass.

These bunnies are six days old. They have not opened their eyes yet.

RABBIT FACTS

NUMBER OF	
KINDS	44 rabbits and hares
COLOR	brownish-gray; pet rabbits can be many colors
LENGTH	up to 24 inches
WEIGHT	up to 11 lbs.
STATUS	common
LIFE SPAN	up to 6 years
ENEMIES	foxes, snakes, eagles, people

sensitive nose to smell friends and enemies

long ears to listen for danger

a European rabbit

strong back legs for hopping and running

PLANT EATER

A rabbit eats mostly grass, clover, and herbs. In winter the rabbit eats bark, twigs, and seeds. Rabbits that live near the sea eat seaweed.

Raccoon

see also: Mammal

A raccoon is a furry mammal. It has black stripes around its tail and a black face mask. Raccoons live near trees and water. They live in North and South America. Raccoons can swim and climb well.

Raccoon families

The female raccoon has as many as three babies. They are called *kits*. The mother feeds the kits milk. She teaches the older kits to fish with their front paws.

In summer, some raccoons live on their own. Some live in small groups. A group is a mother raccoon and her kits. In winter, raccoons crowd together in dens to keep warm.

These kits are staying near their den.

RACCOON FACTS

NUMBER OF KINDS	1
COLOR	gray and black
LENGTH	up to 3 feet
WEIGHT	up to 33 lbs.
STATUS	common
LIFE SPAN	up to 10 years
ENEMIES	people

sharp teeth for tearing food and crushing crab shells

a raccoon

tail for balance while climbing

hands for feeling and gripping

MEAT EATER

Raccoons usually come out at night. They hunt for eggs in trees. They hunt for crabs, frogs, and fish in water. Raccoons are wild animals, but they often live near people. They move into areas where people have their houses. They search through garbage cans for food.

Radio

see also: Communication, Television

Radio is an important way to communicate. Radio uses radio waves. The radio waves are sent from a transmitter to a receiver. Receivers are usually radios like the ones in cars and homes.

The first radio

The first radio was made by Guglielmo Marconi in 1895. Then in 1901, Marconi discovered how to send a radio signal across the Atlantic Ocean. He sent the signal from England to the United States. After a few years, most big ships had radios. A ship with a radio could send a message if it was in trouble. By the 1920s, people were listening to news, music, and entertainment on their own radios.

How radios work

Each radio signal has a different frequency. The frequency is the number of radio waves that arrive in one second. A person is choosing a frequency when he or she chooses to listen to a radio program.

DID YOU KNOW?

Televisions and cellular telephones use radio signals. Communication satellites receive radio signals from one place on Earth. They bounce the signals back to another place on Earth.

This is a radio tower in Australia. Radio towers are very tall so that the signals they send are not blocked by hills or buildings.

This radio receiver is powered by batteries. Small battery radios were first available in 1955.

Railroad

see also: Train, Transportation

A railroad is a track on which trains travel. Railroads connect cities, factories, and ports. They carry people and goods.

The first railroads

The first railroads were built 200 years ago. They had wooden tracks. Horses pulled boxes of coal along the tracks. Then the steam engine was invented. It was powerful. It could work much faster than horses or people. Railroads became longer and connected more places. They carried more people. Today, some railroads go through mountain tunnels. Some railroads even go under the sea.

People and railroads

People could travel a long way very quickly on railroads. Goods could get to places far from where they were made. Fresh food could travel long distances in short amounts of time. Cities and towns grew because they were connected by railroads.

RAILROAD FACTS

FIRST PUBLIC RAILROAD	opened in 1825, between Stockton and Darlington (England)
LONGEST ROUTE	5,860 miles from Moscow to Nakhodka in Russia
BIGGEST STATION	Grand Central Station in New York City has 67 tracks on two levels

The last spike was driven into this track on May 10, 1869. This completed the railroad line that crossed the United States.

This modern, electric-powered train travels at high speeds. The tracks are made especially for high-speed trains.

Rainbow

see also: Color, Light

A rainbow is an arch of seven different colors. A rainbow happens when white sunlight shines through raindrops. The white light is split into different colors. These colors are called the *color spectrum* of light.

How is a rainbow made?

All the colors of a rainbow are in sunlight. Light from the sun is seen as white light. It is really made up of red, orange, yellow, green, blue, indigo, and violet light.

Sunlight bends when it hits a raindrop. Each color of light bends a little bit differently. The colors separate. They form a spectrum.

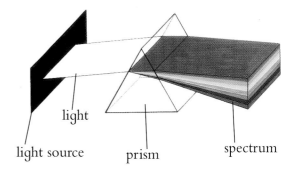

light

light source   prism   spectrum

A raindrop acts like a prism. When the sunlight hits the raindrop, the light is divided into colors.

How to see a rainbow

A rainbow only appears when the sun is low in the sky during a rain shower. To see the rainbow, turn so that the sun is behind you. Look straight ahead. The lower the sun is, the bigger the rainbow arch will be.

This rainbow will fade away when the rain stops falling or when the sun goes behind clouds.

DID YOU KNOW?

You can never find the place where a rainbow comes to the ground. This is because a rainbow is a trick of the light. A rainbow can only be seen from a distance.

Rain Forest

see also: Forest, Plants

Rain forests are very important for the earth. Many different plants and animals live in rain forests. Many of these plants and animals are useful to people. Most rain forests are in hot, wet, tropical areas.

Tropical rain forests

Tropical rain forests have five layers. The bottom layer has small plants, such as mosses and ferns. It also has rich soil made of rotted leaves. Small animals and insects live in the bottom layer. The next layer is shrubs and larger ferns. The third layer is the young trees.

The next layer is the canopy. It is thick and green and about 100 feet high. It is the tops of fully grown trees. The last layer is a few very tall trees. They poke up through the canopy. This layer is called the emergent layer.

This tropical rain forest is along the Amazon River in Brazil. Different plants and animals live in each layer.

Temperate rain forests

There are cool, wet, temperate rain forests in some parts of the United States, Europe, Australia, and Africa. The trees are mainly the type that lose their leaves in winter.

This cool, damp, temperate rain forest is in the state of Washington.

DID YOU KNOW?

Many of the world's rain forests are being cut down. An area nearly as big as Louisiana is cut down every year. If this continues, there will be no rain forests.

Rat

see also: Mammal

A rat is a quick, four-legged mammal. Rats are clever. They can learn to live anywhere. Rats have followed humans around the world. They live in cities and houses where it is warm. They live where there is plenty of food. Rats also live in rural areas. They can spread diseases that can kill people.

Rat families

Rats have many babies. One pair of rats can have hundreds of babies in their lifetime. The female can have a litter three times a year. There might be as many as fourteen babies in each litter. The female feeds the babies milk. The babies look for their own food when they are old enough. In rural areas, rats live in groups called colonies.

RAT FACTS

NUMBER OF	
KINDS	1,082 mice and rats
COLOR	usually brown or gray
LENGTH	up to 20 inches
STATUS	common
LIFE SPAN	up to 5 years
ENEMIES	dogs, cats, people

a brown rat

large flaps protect its sensitive ears

strong, hairless, muscular tail for balance

claws and strong legs for running and climbing

whiskers feel the sid of small spaces to k the rat from getting trapped

This Acacia rat from Botswana, Africa, lives with her family in a tree.

PLANT AND MEAT EATER

Rats have front teeth that never stop growing. The teeth sharpen themselves as they wear down. Rats eat grain, fruit, rubbish, and scraps. They often steal food from humans. They also get into food that is being stored.

Ray

see also: Fish, Sea Life

A ray is a special kind of fish. It does not have fins. A ray has a flat body with wide wings. It swims through the water by flapping its wings. Rays live in oceans around the world. Some rays have poisonous stings on their tails. The stings protect them.

Ray families

Big rays swim alone in the sea. Manta rays are big rays. Smaller rays gather close together in groups. Stingrays are small rays. Rays do not have homes. Some rays spend a lot of time hiding in the sand on the bottom of the sea. Female rays do not lay eggs. They give birth to about ten live babies. The babies look after themselves as soon as they are born.

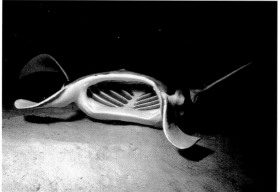

This manta ray has its mouth open. The filter plates inside catch small animals in the water.

RAY FACTS

NUMBER OF KINDS	425
COLOR	different colors on top, white underneath
LENGTH	up to 16 feet
WEIGHT	manta ray—up to 3,000 lbs.
STATUS	common
LIFE SPAN	up to 20 years
ENEMIES	people

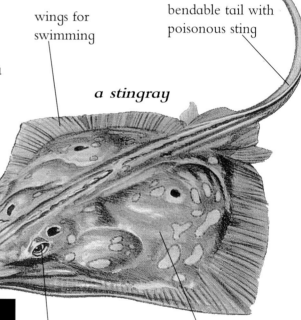

wings for swimming

bendable tail with poisonous sting

a stingray

eyes on the top of the head for seeing things when hiding in sand

flat body for hiding in sand

PLANT AND MEAT EATER

Manta rays eat shrimp, plankton, and small fish that they filter from the water. Stingrays eat sea worms, shellfish, and crabs.

Reptile

see also: Animals

A reptile is a cold-blooded animal with scaly skin. Snakes, crocodiles, lizards, and tortoises are kinds of reptiles. Reptiles live on land and in water. They live all around the world, but not in the coldest places.

Types of reptiles

The four main groups of reptiles are:

Alligators and crocodiles – These are the largest reptiles.

Lizards and snakes – There are more than 5,000 kinds of lizards and snakes around the world. This is the biggest group of reptiles.

Tortoises and turtles – These are protected by their hard shells. The shell of the Galapagos giant tortoise can be 5 feet long.

Tuataras – These are very rare. Tuataras live only on North Island in New Zealand.

INSECT AND MEAT EATER

All reptiles are hunters. They eat meat, fish, and insects. Reptiles do not use their energy to heat their blood, so they do not eat much. Many reptiles can go without food for months or even years.

REPTILE FACTS

NUMBER OF	
KINDS	more than 6,000
LONGEST-LIVED . . .	Marion's tortoise, 152 years
LARGEST	leatherback turtle, 1,658 lbs.

This is a tuatara from New Zealand.

This Wheeler's gecko is a type of lizard. It has sticky pads on its feet. It can crawl up and down vertical surfaces.

Rhinoceros

see also: Mammal

A rhinoceros is a large, horned mammal. A rhinoceros is also called a rhino. Its thick skin is like armor. Three kinds of rhinos live in Asia. These rhinos have only one horn. They are very rare rhinos. Two kinds of rhinos live in Africa. These rhinos have two horns.

RHINOCEROS FACTS

NUMBER OF KINDS	5
COLOR	gray
HEIGHT	up to 7 feet
LENGTH	up to 12 feet
WEIGHT	up to 4,850 lbs.
STATUS	endangered
LIFE SPAN	20 to 50 years
ENEMIES	lions, hyenas, tigers, people

Rhinoceros families

A rhinoceros lives by itself. It lives on grasslands. It shares a waterhole or mud wallow with other rhinos. A male rhino is called a bull. A female is called a cow. A baby is called a calf. A cow has one calf at a time. She looks after her calf for two to five years. Bulls fight over territory, but they let females and calves into their areas.

sensitive ears for hearing enemies and other rhinos

large horn for fighting and protection

upper lip for pulling up plants

thick skin for protection

PLANT EATER

A rhinoceros eats branches, leaves, fruit, grass, and herbs.

This female rhinoceros is feeding her calf. She has a very long horn.

River

see also: Delta, Flood, Valley

A river is a flow of water that drains the land. Rivers carry water from the land to the sea. A small river is called a stream.

Why rivers flow

The water in rivers comes from rain and melting snow. Some rivers begin at a lake or marsh in the mountains. Others start at a spring. A spring is where water flows out from under the ground.

Streams and rivers flow into each other to make bigger rivers. These smaller streams and rivers are called *tributaries.* Rivers wash away soil and rocks. Rivers make valleys.

People and rivers

People use rivers for drinking water and for watering crops. They also use rivers for bathing, washing clothes, fishing, and traveling. Fast-flowing rivers and waterfalls can be used to make electricity.

DID YOU KNOW?

The river with the most flowing water is the Amazon River in South America. The Amazon is nearly 4,000 miles long.

Some rivers make large bends or loops. The loops are called meanders.

People fish in rivers for food and for fun.

Road

see also: Transportation

A road is a pathway used by people to get from one place to another. Some roads follow paths made thousands of years ago. Most roads are new.

The first roads

Early roads were simple paths used by people and animals. They were usually the shortest or easiest way to go from one place to another. These roads were hard, dirt roads. They were made by people's footsteps packing down the dirt. These roads turned to mud when it rained.

The ancient Romans built the first road system. These roads were hard and level. They were easy to use in all weather. They were made for soldiers to walk on. Today's roads are made for wheeled vehicles, such as buses, cars, and trucks.

People and roads

Most people use roads every day. Roads make travel easy, but the traffic can cause air pollution. Roads are also expensive to design, build, and repair.

DID YOU KNOW?

The ancient Roman roads were always built as straight as possible.

ROAD FIRSTS

FIRST RECOGNIZED ROAD...	Persia, 3500 B.C.
FIRST PAVED ROAD..........	England, 1835
FIRST MOTORWAY...........	Italy, 1924

This is a turnpike road in England from long ago. People had to pay to use turnpikes. The money they paid was used to repair the roads.

Some modern road systems are complicated. The roads that go over the top are called overpasses. The roads that go underneath are called underpasses.

Robot

see also: Laser, Space Exploration

A robot is a machine. It works automatically or by remote control. Most robots are used in factories. They do tiresome, heavy, or dangerous jobs.

How robots work
A robot is programmed to do a certain job. This means that the instructions for the job are usually in a computer program. The robot stores the program. Then it will do the same job again and again. The robot's program must be changed if it is to do a different job.

Robots and space exploration
Robots can go on very long journeys through space. They can continue to

One day robots may be as clever as these movie robots. C3PO and R2D2 were in the movie Star Wars.

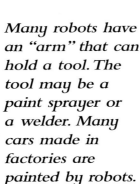

Many robots have an "arm" that can hold a tool. The tool may be a paint sprayer or a welder. Many cars made in factories are painted by robots.

work in places where people would die. Robot space probes have gone to almost every planet in the solar system. They have not gone to Pluto.

DID YOU KNOW?

Scientists are trying to make robots that can be programmed to think. When a computer or robot thinks, it is called "artificial intelligence."

Rocks

see also: Metal, Mining

Rocks are the solid, non-living things that make up the earth. Rocks take many millions of years to form. They are on the ground and under the ground. Rocks are everywhere in the world. There are many different types of rock. Some rocks are hard. Other rocks are soft.

The three kinds of rock

Igneous rock There is no solid rock deep inside the earth. There is only a hot liquid called *magma.* Igneous rocks are formed when magma comes near the surface or erupts from a volcano. The hot magma cools down. It becomes solid. Igneous rocks are usually hard rocks. They do not wear away quickly.

Sedimentary rock These soft rocks were mostly formed in lakes or oceans. Some rocks were made from layers of sand or mud. Other rocks were made from the tiny shells of lake or sea creatures. It took millions of years to press them into rock.

Metamorphic rocks Sedimentary rock turns into metamorphic rock when it is heated and pressed together. Metamorphic rocks are usually harder than sedimentary rocks.

These chalk cliffs are sedimentary rock. They were eroded by the sea.

DID YOU KNOW?

Rocks are made of minerals. Some minerals are metals. Iron, gold, copper, and silver are metals. Other minerals, such as salt, sulphur, and quartz, are not metals.

Slate is a metamorphic rock. It was made from layers of heated mud. Slate can be split and used on roofs.

Romania

see also: Europe

Romania is a country in southeast Europe. It has a coast along the Black Sea. The middle of Romania has mountains. The Danube River flows through the south. The winter weather is cold and dry. The summers are warm. Deer and wild boar live in the big forests.

Living in Romania

About one third of the people work on farms. Farmers grow wheat, corn, sugar beets, and vegetables. They raise herds of cattle and sheep.

Romanians make goods from chemicals, cement, and metals. Pollution from factories is a problem in Romania.

Stories about Count Dracula come from this part of southern Romania called Transylvania.

DID YOU KNOW?

At least 300 kinds of birds live in the delta of the Danube River. Many birds stop there when they fly south for the winter.

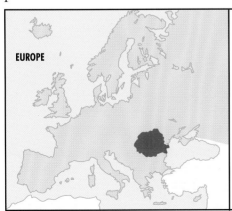

EUROPE

FACT FILE

PEOPLE	Romanians
POPULATION	about 23 million
MAIN LANGUAGE	Romanian
CAPITAL CITY	Bucharest
MONEY	Leu
HIGHEST MOUNTAIN	Mount Moldoveanu—8,349 feet
LONGEST RIVER	Danube River—1,770 miles

Rome, Ancient

see also: Italy, Road

The empire of ancient Rome began with the city of Rome in Italy. Then the Romans took over other lands. They built a huge empire. The ancient Romans are known for their Latin language and their roads.

KEY DATES

753 B.C.	city of Rome begins
250 B.C.	Romans control Italy
250 B.C.–A.D.120	Romans take over more land in Europe, Asia, and North Africa
A.D. 395	Roman Empire splits into two parts

Who ruled ancient Rome?

At first, Rome was ruled by kings. Then the empire grew. It was ruled by a group of people called a Senate. Finally, the empire was ruled by an emperor. He had all the power.

What happened to ancient Rome?

The Roman Empire was at its largest in A.D.120. It was too big to be controlled from Rome. So it split into two parts. The Roman Empire became smaller as other countries and empires formed.

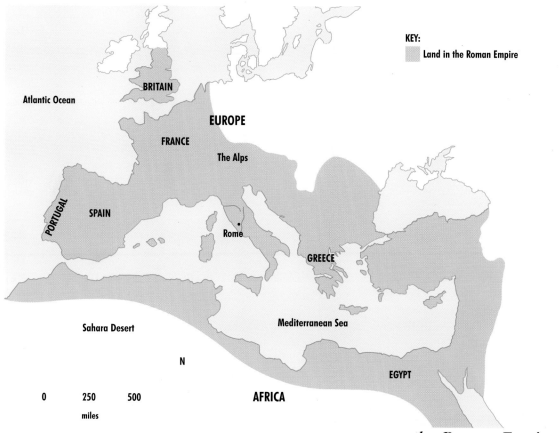

KEY:
Land in the Roman Empire

BRITAIN
Atlantic Ocean
EUROPE
FRANCE
The Alps
PORTUGAL
SPAIN
Rome
GREECE
Mediterranean Sea
Sahara Desert
N
EGYPT
0   250   500
miles
AFRICA

the Roman Empire

Root

see also: Plants

The roots of a plant are the parts that usually grow under the ground. Roots take in water. They hold the plant in the soil.

The life of a root

The root is usually the first part of a plant to grow from a seed. The tip of the root pushes down through the soil. Some plants have a large main root called a *taproot.* Other plants produce a network of roots. These roots grow in all directions.

Many vegetables are roots. Carrots, sweet potatoes, beets, cassava, and yams are roots. These roots store food for the plant.

All plant roots help to hold soil in place. They keep the soil from being blown away by wind or washed away by rain.

DID YOU KNOW?

Some roots never go underground. Aerial roots take in water from the air. Orchids have aerial roots to hold onto bigger plants. Ivy has many small climbing roots to cling to trees and walls.

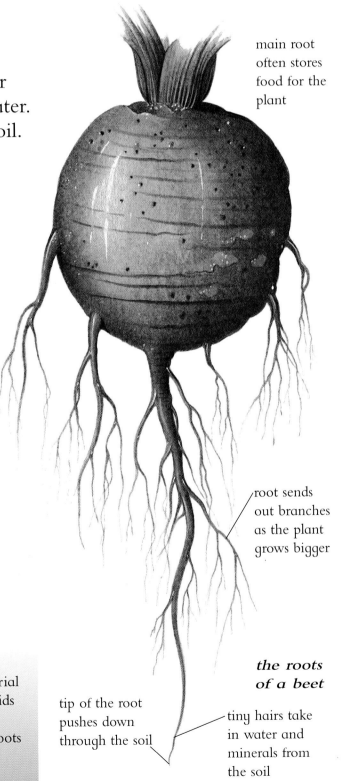

main root often stores food for the plant

root sends out branches as the plant grows bigger

the roots of a beet

tip of the root pushes down through the soil

tiny hairs take in water and minerals from the soil

Russia

see also: Asia, Europe

Russia is a very large country. Part of it is in Europe. Part of it is in Asia. The Ural Mountains divide Europe from Asia. The north of Russia is inside the Arctic Circle. The south is dry and much warmer.

Living in Russia

The best farmland in Russia is in the west. Farmers in the west grow wheat, potatoes, and other crops. They also raise cattle. There is mining for coal and metals, and drilling for oil and gas. Factory workers make everything from matchsticks to microwaves. Most people in the cities live in apartment buildings. About one-fourth of the Russian people live in the rural areas. Some Russians who live in the forests still live in traditional wooden huts called *izba*.

Many different groups of people live in Russia. Each group has its own customs, music, and dancing.

St. Basil's Cathedral is in Moscow's Red Square. It is famous for its onion-shaped roofs. A big May Day parade is held in Red Square each year.

DID YOU KNOW?

Russia and fourteen smaller countries were called the Soviet Union until 1991.

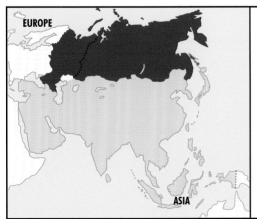

EUROPE

ASIA

FACT FILE

PEOPLE	Russians
POPULATION	about 160 million
MAIN LANGUAGE	Russian
CAPITAL CITY	Moscow
MONEY	Ruble
HIGHEST MOUNTAIN	Elbrus—18,517 feet
LONGEST RIVER	Yenisey-Angara—3,445 miles

Rwanda

see also: Africa

Rwanda is a small country in the middle of Africa. There are mountains and forests. It is warm and wet all year round.

Living in Rwanda

Most families in Rwanda live in small houses that they build themselves. These houses have mud walls. The roofs are made from the leaves of banana trees. Most houses also have a small garden where the family grows its own food. They grow bananas, sweet potatoes, and a plant called *cassava*. The roots of the cassava plant are used to make flour. Some farmers grow coffee and tea to sell to other countries

There are two main tribes, or groups, in Rwanda. They are called the Hutu and the Tutsi. Fights started in 1994 between the Hutu and the Tutsi. Many Rwandans have been killed in the fighting.

Rwanda has some of the tallest and shortest people on Earth. The Tutsi dancers shown here are very tall. The Twa people, known as Pygmies, also live in Rwanda. They are some of the smallest people in the world.

DID YOU KNOW?

Mountain gorillas in Rwanda are an endangered species. Very few of these gorillas are left because of armies fighting and illegal hunters who kill gorillas.

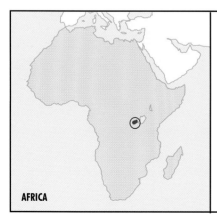

AFRICA

FACT FILE

PEOPLE	Rwandans
POPULATION	about 6 million
CAPITAL CITY	Kigali
MAIN LANGUAGES	Kinyarwanda and French
MONEY	Rwandan franc
HIGHEST MOUNTAIN	Mount Karisimbi–14,792 feet
LONGEST RIVER	Kagera–248 miles

R

Saudi Arabia

see also: Asia

Saudi Arabia is a country in the Middle East. Most of Saudi Arabia is a hot desert. It has sand dunes, stones, and bare rock. Snakes, lizards, rats, and wild cats live in the desert. There are mountains in the west.

Living in Saudi Arabia

About half of the people work in farming. Farmers grow wheat, bananas, and dates in areas where there is water. Some Saudis have herds of goats and camels. There is oil in the rocks under Saudi Arabia. The oil is sold to other countries.

Almost everyone in Saudi Arabia is a follower of the religion of Islam. The holy city of Islam is Mecca in Saudi Arabia. Followers of Islam try to make a special journey to Mecca once in their lives. This journey is called a *pilgrimage*.

At this market in Saudi Arabia all goods of one type are sold together. Here leather goods are on sale.

DID YOU KNOW?

The Saudi flag has Arabic writing on it. The Saudi flag is one of only a few national flags with words.

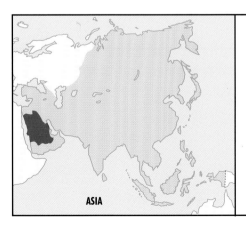

ASIA

FACT FILE

PEOPLE	Saudis
POPULATION	about 18 million
CAPITAL CITY	Riyadh
MAIN LANGUAGE	Arabic
MONEY	Saudi riyal
HIGHEST MOUNTAIN	Jabal Sawda—10,283 feet

Scorpion

see also: Invertebrate

A scorpion is a small animal. It has two large claws on its front legs and it has six other legs. A scorpion has a curved tail. The tail has a sharp stinger on the end. Scorpions are hunters. They live mainly in warm parts of the world. The scorpion is from the same group of animals as the spider.

Scorpion families

Female scorpions have lots of babies. They look like tiny, see-through, adult scorpions. Scorpions hide under rocks or in holes in the daytime. They like cool, damp places out of the sun's heat.

SCORPION FACTS

NUMBER OF	
KINDS	more than 1,400
COLOR	black or brown
LENGTH	half inch to 7 inches
STATUS	rare
WEIGHT	much less than one ounce
ENEMIES	owls, frogs, snakes, rats

a thick-tailed scorpion

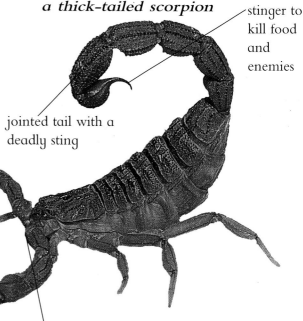

stinger to kill food and enemies

jointed tail with a deadly sting

strong claws for grabbing food

jaws for tearing food into small pieces

Babies ride on the mother's back for about a year. Then they look after themselves.

INSECT AND MEAT EATER

Scorpions hunt at night. They use their poisonous stings to kill insects, centipedes, spiders, and lizards. Scorpions can live in the driest places. They can go without water for months. They can live without food for more than a year.

Scotland

see also: United Kingdom, Europe

Scotland is one of the four main parts of the United Kingdom. Mountains cover much of Scotland. There are many long inlets and islands around the west coast.

Every year the Scottish Highland Games include a variety of sports. This sportsman wearing a tartan kilt is throwing the hammer.

Living in Scotland

The two biggest cities in Scotland are Glasgow and Edinburgh. Not many people live in the mountains or on the islands. Some Scots make a living by farming and fishing. Others look after the tourists in hotels.

Scottish people sometimes wear clothes made from a special patterned, woolen cloth. It is called *tartan*. Each family, or clan, has its own pattern and colors.

DID YOU KNOW?

Loch Ness is a lake in the Scottish Highlands. It is famous for the sightings of a large animal called the Loch Ness Monster. Some people believe the animal is real. Other people do not think it exists at all.

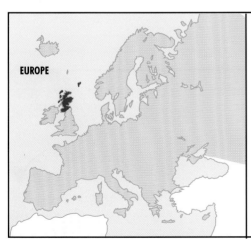

EUROPE

FACT FILE

PEOPLE	Scots, Scottish
POPULATION	about 5 million
MAIN LANGUAGES	English and Scottish Gaelic
CAPITAL CITY	Edinburgh
LARGEST CITY	Glasgow
MONEY	Pound sterling
HIGHEST MOUNTAIN	Ben Nevis–4,411 feet
LONGEST RIVER	Tay River–120 miles

Sculpture

see also: Art

Sculpture is works of art, such as statues and other objects. A sculpture can show a real object. It can also be an image that tries to show a feeling or an idea. A person who makes sculptures is called a *sculptor*.

Making sculptures

Sculpture can be made of almost any material. Very hard materials, such as stone or metal, are often used. Hard materials last a long time. Stone and wood are chipped and carved. Metal, plaster, and plastic sculptures are usually made by pouring liquid into a mold.

DID YOU KNOW?

The earliest known sculptures are about 30 thousand years old. One of the oldest sculptures is a carving of a horse. It was found in a cave in Germany.

This huge wooden sculpture of a chair is on display in a forest. It is made from wood grown in the forest.

A sculpture of a human or animal figure is called a statue. *Statues like this were sometimes used as columns on buildings in ancient Greece and Rome.*

Sea Anemone

see also: Sea Life

A sea anemone is a sea animal with a soft body. It has no bones. Different sea anemones live in shallow seas and rockpools near the seashore. They are found all over the world. Sea anemones are members of the same group of animals as jellyfish and corals.

Sea anemone families

Some sea anemones lay eggs to make baby anemones. Other kinds make more anemones by dividing off parts of their own bodies. A sucker keeps the sea anemone stuck in the same place. This is where it will spend most of its life.

SEA ANEMONE FACTS

NUMBER OF KINDS	more than 9,000
COLOR	all colors
LENGTH	1 to 3 inches
STATUS	common
LIFE SPAN	up to hundreds of years
ENEMIES	sea slugs, fish

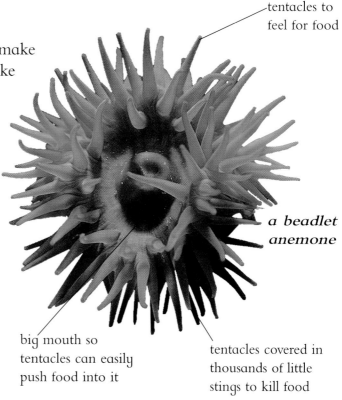

tentacles to feel for food

a beadlet anemone

big mouth so tentacles can easily push food into it

tentacles covered in thousands of little stings to kill food

This green sea anemone is eating a crab.

MEAT EATER

Sea anemones eat animals such as shrimp and small fish. They use the stingers on the tentacles around their mouths to catch and kill animals. The tentacles push the food into its open mouth.

Sea Horse

see also: Fish

A sea horse is a very strange fish. Its head looks like a horse's head. It has a curved tail and a long sucking mouth. Sea horses live in warm seas all over the world.

Sea horse families

Female sea horses lay eggs in the male sea horse. He has a special pouch to hold the eggs. When the eggs hatch, the male sea horse opens the pouch. The babies swim out.

MEAT EATER

Sea horses are too slow to chase and to catch food. So they hold perfectly still. They wait for food to come to them. When small shrimp or little fish swim past, the sea horse sucks them up like a vacuum cleaner.

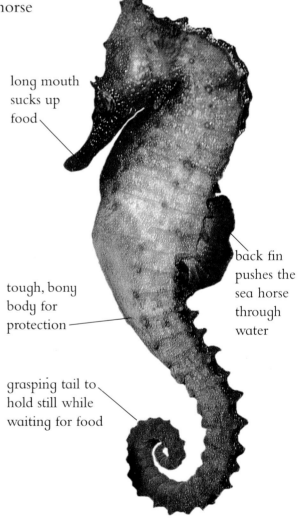

long mouth sucks up food

back fin pushes the sea horse through water

tough, bony body for protection

grasping tail to hold still while waiting for food

a White's sea horse

These newly hatched, short-snouted seahorses are able to swim away as soon as they are born.

Sea Life

see also: Coral, Fish

Most of the world is covered by the sea. Many plants and animals live or feed in the sea. Most sea life is near the top of the water. This is where there is plenty of light. Some creatures live in the deep sea where it is dark.

Some of the creatures that live deep in the sea look very strange. This hatchetfish lights up.

Living in the sea

Plants and animals need oxygen to live. Most sea animals take oxygen from the water. Sea plants use sunlight to make oxygen and food. Seabirds and mammals that live in the sea breathe the air at the surface of the water.

Most sea life is made of tiny creatures and plants called *plankton.* They live in the sunlight near the top of the sea. Many sea animals eat plankton. Even the largest whales eat plankton. Fish are in all the seas around the world.

Most fish stay near the surface, but some live on the bottom of the sea. Mollusks, such as shellfish and octopus, sit on the bottom of the sea. Crustaceans, such as crabs and shrimp, also live on the bottom. They eat bits of dead plants and animals that sink.

DID YOU KNOW?

Coral reefs are found in shallow, warm water. Many different creatures live on and around coral reefs. Corals reefs are made by millions of tiny coral polyps.

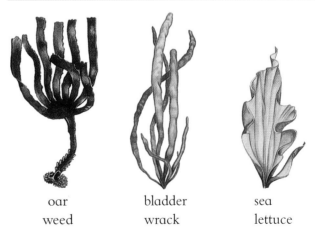

oar weed   bladder wrack   sea lettuce

There are 7,000 kinds of seaweed. They look very different in shape, size, and color. Seaweed can be used for food, fertilizer, and medicines.

Sea Lion

see also: Mammals, Sea Life

A sea lion is a mammal. It lives in the sea. It comes onto beaches to have its babies. Sea lions live in the Pacific and Atlantic Oceans. They can move faster than a person on land. They can swim as fast as 25 miles per hour.

SEA LION FACTS

NUMBER OF KINDS	5
COLOR	light brown
LENGTH	up to 7 feet
WEIGHT	up to 600 lbs.
STATUS	common
LIFE SPAN	up to 15 years
ENEMIES	killer whales, people

Sea lion families

A male sea lion is called a bull. A female sea lion is called a cow. A baby sea lion is called a pup. A bull marks out a territory. It gets as many cows as possible to stay there. Each female has one pup at a time. She feeds the pup on milk for about six months. Then it is old enough to hunt for its own food.

good eyes for seeing food

ears to listen underwater for food

long, smooth body to help push through the water

a South American sea lion

back flippers to swim straight or turn quickly in the water

strong front flippers for swimming fast

These Steller's sea lions are gathering on a beach to mate.

MEAT EATER

A sea lion eats fish, squid, and octopus. It can see very well. It chases its prey through the water.

Sea Urchin

see also: Sea Life

A sea urchin is a ball-shaped animal. It has a hard spiny skin. Sea urchins live in seas all over the world. They are one of the very oldest kinds of sea creatures.

Sea urchin families

Sea urchins lay eggs. They send the eggs floating off into the sea. The eggs hatch into tiny sea urchins. Adult sea urchins do not take care of the eggs or the babies.

Sea urchins move around on hundreds of special tube feet. Each tube has suckers on it. Sea urchins use the suckers to grip onto underwater rocks.

SEA URCHIN FACTS

NUMBER OF KINDS	700
COLOR	all colors
SIZE	2 to 12 inches across
STATUS	common
LIFE SPAN	about 10 years
ENEMIES	fish, people

sharp spines protect against enemies; some sea urchins have poisonous spines

a sea urchin

spines that grow again if they are snapped off

These white sea urchins are eating a skin that was shed by a lobster.

PLANT AND MEAT EATER

A sea urchin uses the five moving pincers around its mouth to scrape up algae and small animals, such as coral.

Seabird

see also: Birds, Gull

A seabird is any kind of bird that feeds in the sea. Gulls and terns are seabirds. Some ducks, geese, and swans are seabirds, too. Some seabirds, like the albatross, spend much of their lives at sea. They only visit land to breed.

Seabird families

Different seabirds have different kinds of family life. All seabirds lay their eggs on land. Most seabirds have nests. Some nests are in trees or cliffs. Other nests are on the beach or in the grass. Some seabirds nest in burrows in the ground. Both male and female seabirds feed their chicks.

SEABIRD FACTS

COLOR	mostly white, gray, or black
LENGTH	10 inches to 4 feet
WEIGHT	2 ounces to 26 lbs.
STATUS	most are common
LIFE SPAN	5 to 30 years
ENEMIES	land animals that eat eggs and attack chicks

MEAT EATER

Most seabirds eat fish, squid, or shellfish. Some seabirds can dive deep into the sea. Other seabirds pick up food close to the surface.

The puffin has a large and colorful bill. The bill can hold many small fish at one time.

The cormorant dives from the sky into the water to catch fish. Then it dries its wings before it flies again.

Seal

see also: Mammal, Sea Lion

The seal is a mammal. It lives in the sea. There are many kinds of seals all over the world. Many seals live in cold water. Some live in warm water. Fur seals have thick fur. Most other seals have shiny, waterproof short hair.

Seal families

A male seal is called a bull. A female seal is called a cow. A baby seal is called a pup. Bulls are usually much bigger than cows. The bulls usually swim to land in the spring before the cows do. Each bull chooses a bit of land. Then he tries to get cows to move onto his land.

A cow has only one pup each year. Pups are born with special furry coats to keep them warm. Cows feed their pups on milk until the pups can hunt for fish and squid.

SEAL FACTS

NUMBER OF KINDS	19
COLOR	gray or brown
LENGTH	some kinds up to 16 feet
WEIGHT	some kinds up to 6,000 lbs.
STATUS	some are rare
LIFE SPAN	up to 38 years
ENEMIES	killer whales, people

big eyes for seeing in murky water

waterproof fur and thick blubber to keep warm in cold water

flippers for swimming

a Southern fur seal

MEAT EATER

Most seals eat fish, shellfish, and squid. The leopard seal eats penguins. Seals can dive very deep under water to chase food.

These harp seal pups have white fur. They cannot be seen in the snow.

Seasons

see also: Climate, Weather

Seasons are the different times of the year. Each season has its own kind of weather. The seasons happen at about the same time every year.

The four seasons
Some places have four seasons: spring, summer, autumn, and winter.

Spring The days get longer. Plants begin to grow. Many farmers sow their seeds. Some animals mate in the spring. Other animals give birth.

Summer It is warm. There is plenty of light. The days are long. Plants grow and make food for animals. Many animals raise their young.

Autumn The days get shorter. Crops ripen and are harvested.

Winter It is colder. The days are short. The nights are long. Most plants stop growing. Some plants lose their leaves. There is less food for animals. Some animals hibernate. Other animals migrate to warmer places.

In autumn, the leaves of some types of trees change from green to bright red, orange, and yellow.

Some places that do not have four seasons have dry and rainy seasons. This shows a storm during the rainy season in Malaysia.

DID YOU KNOW?

Some places have no seasons at all. The days are always about the same length near the equator. This part of the world is hot and wet. Tropical rainforests are always hot and wet. Some deserts are always hot and dry.

Seed

see also: Crop, Plants

The seed is the part of a plant that may take root in the ground. It may grow into a new plant. Nuts and grains are seeds. Fruits have seeds inside them.

The life of a seed

A seed comes from a flower. The seeds inside the flower swell and ripen as the flower's petals wilt and die. Birds, animals, water, and wind help to scatter different kinds of seeds. A new plant may grow when a seed falls to the ground and starts to grow in the soil.

A seed stores food. People and animals eat the seeds of many plants. Nuts are seeds protected by hard shells. Grain is the seed of wheat. Grain is ground into flour to make bread and pasta. Rice, beans, peas, and sweetcorn are all seeds. They can be cooked and eaten.

Stage 1 The root pushes its way out of the seed into the soil.

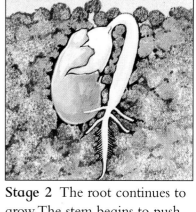

Stage 2 The root continues to grow. The stem begins to push its way out of the soil.

Stage 3 The stem grows above the soil. Leaves start to grow out of the seed.

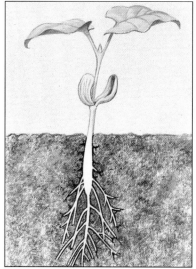

Stage 4 The root, stem, and leaves grow into a little plant.

These pictures show the four stages of the growth of a seed into a plant.

Shark

see also: Fish

A shark is a fish. Different kinds of sharks live in oceans and seas all over the world. Most sharks live in warm water. The great white shark, the blue shark, the tiger shark, and the leopard shark sometimes attack people.

Shark families

Little is known about shark families. The female shark gives birth to babies. They swim away on their own. Some kinds of sharks have as many as 80 babies at a time.

Young sharks are called pups. They stay close to the coasts. They only go into deep water after they have grown bigger.

SHARK FACTS

NUMBER OF KINDS	340
COLOR	white, yellow, gray, or blue
LENGTH	usually up to 20 feet (whale shark 66 feet long)
WEIGHT	usually up to 2,650 lbs. (whale shark 15,400 lbs.)
STATUS	great white shark is rare
LIFE SPAN	about 35 years
ENEMIES	big sharks that eat smaller sharks; people

high back fin to turn around quickly

long side fins move to keep the shark level and to keep it from sinking

long tail swishes to build up speed

a great white shark

sharp teeth to hold and cut food

MEAT EATER

A shark eats fish. It catches them with its sharp teeth. Some sharks can smell blood in the water. Big sharks, like the tiger shark, will eat turtles and seals. The whale shark is the world's biggest shark. It eats only tiny creatures called krill and plankton.

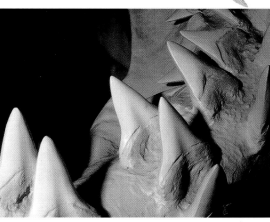

The great white shark has two rows of sharp teeth.

Sheep

see also: Mammal

A sheep is a mammal. It has a long, warm, woolly coat. It has special feet so it can live on mountains and hills. There are many different types of sheep. Farmers around the world keep sheep. Sheep are raised for their meat, milk, and wool.

SHEEP FACTS

NUMBER OF KINDS	914
COLOR	usually white or brown
HEIGHT	up to 5 feet
LENGTH	up to 5 feet
WEIGHT	up to 300 lbs.
STATUS	common
LIFE SPAN	up to 20 years
ENEMIES	wolves, eagles, crows

some rams have horns for fighting

wool coat to keep warm

soft, split hooves for good balance when walking on rocks and hard ground

a sheep

Sheep families

A male sheep is called a ram. A female sheep is called an ewe. A baby sheep is called a lamb. An ewe has one or two lambs each year. Ewes, lambs, and one or two rams live in a large group called a flock. The female lambs stay in the flock after they have grown up. Most male lambs raised by farmers are sold for meat.

PLANT EATER

A sheep eats grass and the leaves of small bushes. Some sheep have very tough mouths. This helps them to eat prickly leaves and thorns.

This flock of Merino sheep is grazing in New Zealand. There are 58 million sheep in New Zealand. There are only about 3 million people.

Ship

see also: Barge, Port, Transportation, Waterway

A ship is a vessel that travels over the sea. Some ships carry goods. These are called cargo ships. Giant ships called tankers carry oil. Many countries have ships. They use the ships for protection or in wars.

The first ships

The first known ships were built in Egypt about 6,000 years ago. The first sailing ships were built from wood or bundles of reeds. Ships have had engines for the past 150 years. Ships with engines are faster and more reliable than sailing ships. Today, big ships are built from steel.

People and ships

Ships are the easiest way to send large amounts of goods from one country to another. Almost all long-distance travel used to be by ship. Now much of this traveling is done by airplane.

DID YOU KNOW?

The first settlers who traveled from Europe to the United States and Australia made the journey by ship. Today, most passenger ships are used for vacations. Other ships called *ferries* travel shorter distances. Ferries carry people and vehicles.

SHIP FIRSTS

FIRST SEA-GOING SHIP	ancient Egypt, 4000 B.C.
FIRST SHIP TO GO AROUND THE WORLD	The Victoria in 1522
FIRST STEAM-POWERED SHIP TO CROSS THE ATLANTIC OCEAN	The Savannah in 1819

This modern oil tanker is guided into port by smaller boats called tugboats.

The first ships were small. Wooden ships and boats like this one are still used for fishing in India.

Sikhism

Sikhism is a world religion. Its followers are called Sikhs. The word *Sikh* means "learner." The Sikh religion began in northwest India and part of Pakistan. It grew from the teachings of Guru Nanak. He lived nearly 600 years ago.

Beliefs and teachings

Guru Nanak was born in 1469 in the Punjab. He believed that God told him to show people how to follow a simple faith. Nine other gurus followed Guru Nanak. The tenth guru put all the teachings into a book. The book is called the *Guru Granth Sahib.*

Sikhs believe in one God. They believe that God is neither a man nor a woman. They believe that God has no color or rank. Sikhs think about the meaning of God. They try to live their lives with honesty, hard work, and caring.

The book of teachings, Guru Granth Sahib, *is kept on a throne. It is looked after by a special person called a granthi.*

Sikhism today

There are about 20 million Sikhs all over the world. Most live in India. Sikhs pray at home and in Sikh temples. The temples are called *gurdwaras*. Food is also served in the *gurdwaras*. Festivals called *gurpurbs* mark the anniversaries of the ten Sikh gurus.

Food prepared in the kitchen of the Sikh temple is served at a Sikh wedding.

DID YOU KNOW?

Sikhs have five special symbols called *The Five Ks.* The symbols are worn by the Khalsa. They are groups of devout Sikhs.

Singapore

see also: Asia, Port

Singapore is a very small country. It is in southeast Asia. Most of Singapore is on one big island. The weather is always hot and wet. The forests have monkeys and many types of butterflies.

Living in Singapore

Most people work in banks or other office jobs. Many women make parts for computers. Some people have jobs in the docks at the port.

People from China, Malaysia, India, and other countries have come to live in Singapore. Each group has its own festivals. Street parades with dragons and lanterns celebrate the Chinese New Year.

There are many modern buildings in Singapore.

DID YOU KNOW?

The port of Singapore is the largest port in the world.

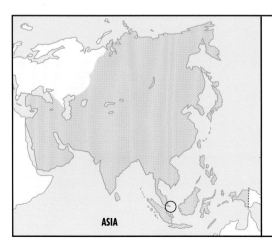

ASIA

FACT FILE

PEOPLE . . . . Singaporean

POPULATION . . . . about 3 million

MAIN LANGUAGES . . English, Malay, Chinese, Tamil

CAPITAL CITY . . . . Singapore City

MONEY . . . . Singapore dollar

HIGHEST POINT . . . . . Bukit Tamah Hill—578 feet

Skeleton

see also: Human Body, Vertebrate

A skeleton is the framework of bones that holds up an animal. A skeleton protects the important organs. It helps the animal to move.

The human skeleton

The human body has more than 200 bones joined together to make a skeleton. Living cells make new bones as humans grow. Many of the bones of young babies are not hard. They bend easily. The bones of adults become more brittle. They break more easily.

Joints and moving

The skeleton must have joints to move. Some joints between bones are like the hinges of a door. The bones move but stay fixed together. Ligaments are like strong strings. They hold the bones together at the joints. Tendons are like ligaments. They join the muscles to the bones. Bones are moved when muscles pull on them.

DID YOU KNOW?

Some animals have a skeleton on the outside. This is called an exoskeleton. Shells are exoskeletons. An exoskeleton cannot grow. An exoskeleton is shed as the animal gets bigger. Then the animal forms another exoskeleton.

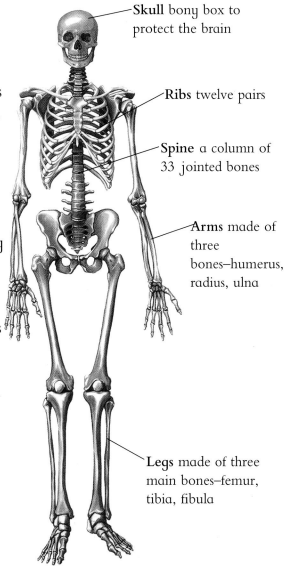

Skull bony box to protect the brain

Ribs twelve pairs

Spine a column of 33 jointed bones

Arms made of three bones–humerus, radius, ulna

Legs made of three main bones–femur, tibia, fibula

the human skeleton

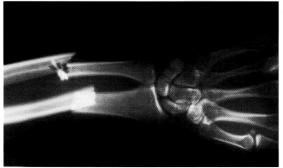

This X-ray shows an arm with two broken bones.

Skunk

see also: Mammal

The skunk is a mammal. It hunts at night. It lives in North America. A skunk is black and white. These colors warn off other animals. A skunk sprays a horrible-smelling liquid on its enemies or when it is frightened.

Skunk families

A skunk often lives in a woodpile. Its home is called a den. Sometimes it shares its den with a fox or a raccoon. Several skunks will share a den in winter. They sleep or rest for several months.

The female skunk gives birth to as many as ten babies. The babies are called kits. She feeds them milk. Kits stay with their mother even after they are old enough to hunt.

glands under the tail spray a bad smelling liquid at enemies

Kits stay close to their den or their mother when they are young.

SKUNK FACTS

NUMBER OF KINDS	13
COLOR	black and white
LENGTH	18 inches plus tail
WEIGHT	up to 7 lbs.
STATUS	common
LIFE SPAN	about 7 years
ENEMIES	bobcats, owls, people

fur and fluffy tail to keep warm

sharp claws for digging up food

a skunk

PLANT, INSECT, AND MEAT EATER

A skunk digs in the soil to find insects. It looks for grasshoppers and beetles. It also digs up worms, roots, and fungi. A skunk will also claw fish out of the water.

Slovakia

see also: Europe, Czech Republic

Slovakia is a country in central Europe. It has many mountains with forests. The flat land in the south has hot temperatures. Winters are cold. Summers are warm.

Living in Slovakia

Most Slovakians live in the country. Farmers grow grapes, sugar beets, corn, and wheat. Many people work in factories. They make ceramics and machinery.

There are many traditional foods in Slovakia. The spice called paprika is cooked with beef and chicken. Pancakes are filled with chocolate sauce.

Slovakia is famous for making musical instruments. Folk music festivals are held in eastern Slovakia. Local musicians perform at pop music festivals in Bratislava.

St. Martin's Cathedral is one of the tallest buildings in Bratislava.

DID YOU KNOW?

Slovakia and the Czech Republic once formed the country of Czechoslovakia. Slovakia became independent in 1993.

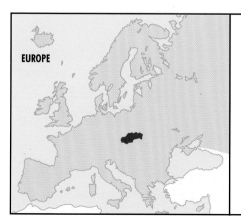

EUROPE

FACT FILE

PEOPLE............Slovaks, Slovakians

POPULATION ....about 5 million

MAIN LANGUAGE ..Slovak

CAPITAL CITY......Bratislava

MONEY............Koruna

HIGHEST POINT....Gerlachovský Stít–8,710 feet

LONGEST RIVER....Danube River–1,770 miles

Slovenia

see also: Yugoslavia

Slovenia is a country in southeast Europe. There are hills, mountains, and many forests. Summers are warm. Winters are cold. The mountains have heavy snow.

Living in Slovenia

Half the people in Slovenia live in the cities. They work in offices and factories. They mine for coal, lead, zinc, and mercury. Farmers grow cereals, potatoes, and fruit. Some farmers raise sheep, goats, and cattle.

The mountains are popular with tourists. Many people go to the mountains to ski.

A favorite meal in Slovenia is beans and pork. It is cooked with sauerkraut. Sauerkraut is chopped, pickled cabbage. Slovenes enjoy pastries filled with cheese, apples, walnuts, and poppy seeds. The pastries are called *gibanica*.

At some weddings, women wear highly decorated costumes and embroidered hats.

DID YOU KNOW?

Slovene, the language of Slovenia, has 40 different local forms. Different forms of the same language are called dialects.

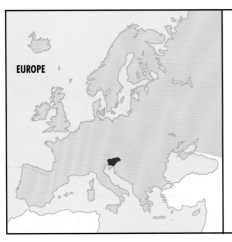

EUROPE

FACT FILE

PEOPLE	Slovenes, Slovenians
POPULATION	2 million
MAIN LANGUAGE	Slovene
CAPITAL CITY	Ljubljana
MONEY	Tolar
HIGHEST MOUNTAIN	Mount Triglav–9,396 feet
LONGEST RIVER	Sava River–584 miles